MAX AND MYRON
Learn BIG & Small
Short & Tall

WRITTEN BY
Wendy VanHatten

R David Kryder

ILLUSTRATED BY
Corie Barloggi

First Printing, January 2014

Published by
WenDa Publishing

Printed in the United States of America

Ginger Marks
Layout by
DocUmeant Designs

www.DocUmeantDesigns.com

ISBN13 978-0-9891192-4-5
ISBN10 0-9891192-4-6

For bulk order pricing contact
customercare@vanhattenwritingservices.com

Dedication

When we first started writing the *Max and Myron* series of books, our inspiration for Myron came from my cat … Myron. For all of his 17 years, he acted like he understood whatever I was saying, he seemed to know my moods, and he cared about what I was doing … most of the time. In the books *Max and Myron*, Max tells his cat, Myron, about his day at school and what he learned. Myron understands and responds as only a cat can. Now, Myron is no longer with us … 17 years is a long time in cat years.

It's hard not having Myron around. But, he will live forever in our books. And … we know he is still listening to us as we write. Thanks, Myron, for all of your inspiration.

Dear Parents, Educators, and Children:

Welcome to the *Max and Myron* series. These books are about a boy and his cat. The authors have written them in a manner to teach both reading and social skills for young children.

The *Max and Myron* series is designed for young readers who:

- Are learning to read in a left to right progression

- Are recognizing sight words

- Are learning new words

- Are recognizing beginning and ending sounds

- Are discovering new words by using pictures as clues

- Are learning by interacting in the conversations as Max talks to Myron

The *Teaching Guides for Children* provides sentence frames. These sentence frames can be used to extend the reader's vocabulary and sentence usage capability.

A *High Frequency Word List* is included in every book. This high frequency word list facilitates the young reader's word recognition and serves as a ready review tool after the book is finished.

A *New Word List* provides words that may be new to the reader's vocabulary.

Critical Thinking Questions promote thinking beyond the story. These can help the reader reflect on real life issues.

Reading with a child is a great beginning . . . enjoy.

High Frequency Word List

On	We
Can	It
Be	And
Not	Is
About	The

New Vocabulary Word List

Big	Skinny
Tall	Teased
Short	Body
Small	Biggest
Shapes	Neighborhood
Sizes	Person
Fat	

Sentence Frames

It is not nice to tease a person about _____

Today, in school, I learned about _____

I say please when I _____

I say thank you when I _____

Critical Thinking Questions

Critical Thinking Questions promote thinking. They allow children to think about the story in depth. They allow children to reflect on what they read. They allow children to reflect on real life situations.

1. What did Max learn in school today?
2. Why is it not nice to tease a person about their body size?
3. Describe how you look.
4. Describe how Myron looks.
5. Describe how Max looks.
6. What would you say to someone who was teased about their body size?

7. How does Dad look?

8. How does Mom look?

9. What does Max want to learn about in school tomorrow?

10. What does Myron want Max to learn about in school?

*Make sure children are giving answers to the questions using complete sentences.

I'm home from school
Myron, where are you?

I'm here on the rug.

Do you know what I learned about in school today?

No. Did you learn
about cats?

No, Myron. I learned today
that people can come in
all shapes and sizes.

Cats can come in all shapes and sizes, too.

People can be tall or short.

People can be fat or skinny.

Cats can be fat or

skinny, too.

I also learned that people get teased about being tall or short and fat or skinny.

It's not nice to tease
about someone's
body size.

You are right, Myron. It is not nice to tease someone about their body size.

It is not nice to tease anyone about anything.

My friend is tall. She is the tallest person in our class.

I know a big cat. He's the biggest cat in our neighborhood.

I like my tall friend. I do not tease her about being tall.

I'm glad you don't tease her
about being tall.

My teacher said we should not tease others about the size of their body.

Teasing makes a person feel bad. It hurts their feelings.

Teasing someone about their body size is not nice.

No one should tease about someone's body size.

It is not important if a person is big or small. It is not important if a person is short or tall.

It is not important if a cat is big or small. It is not important if a cat is short or tall.

What is important is what a person says
and how a
person acts.

What is important is how a cat purrs and how a cat acts.

Mom is tall and skinny. She is perfect the way she is!

You are right, Max. Mom is perfect.

Dad is big and tall. Dad is perfect the way he is.

You are right. Dad is perfect!

Myron, you are small. You are
perfect the way you are.

Max, you are big. You are perfect the way you are.

School is fun. I like learning new things.

I wish I could go to school, too.

Let's go ask Mom for treats.

Let's say please when we ask. Let's say thank you after Mom gives us treats.

What do you think I will learn in school tomorrow?

Maybe you will learn about cats.

Rave Reviews

"It is important to talk with small children about different body sizes and teach them acceptance at a young age. As children grow older they start to become insecure with their body image. Instilling that all different shapes and sizes of people are acceptable will help build confidence in themselves and teach them kindness toward others no matter their body size."

Eileen Neufled
Kindergarten Teacher
Suisun Elementary School
Fairfield, California

"The series of books about *Max and Myron* continues to inspire my class and my grandchildren. The books are easy to read and convey a clear, concise message about how to treat one another. This book about body size and not judging others by how they look is an especially important topic, which is handled in a very loving and inspiring way. Thank you to Wendy for writing it and to Corie for so skillfully illustrating these books!"

Thanks for being you!!

Louise Craig
4th Grade
Suisun Elementary School
Fairfield, California

Meet the Authors

The ***Max and Myron Series*** grew out of a love for animals combined with a passion for teaching ethical behavior. Having lived and taught on all six inhabited continents, he has experienced many shades of behavior – civil and uncivil. Although an ***Intellectual Property Rights Specialist,*** he has taught topics as diverse as ***English As A Second Language, The Holocaust***, ***Applied Mathematics for Auto Technicians,*** and ***Ethics In The Workplace*** Kryder and his wife Patti live in the Santa Cruz River Valley of Southern Arizona with their German Shepherd ***Lady***.

R David Kryder was born on a family farm in Northwest Ohio, as the fourth of seven sons. Speaking with animals – like Max does with Myron – is natural for him. Animals are great listeners. By speaking with them, we work through issues we face.

Wendy VanHatten is a published author, editor, educator, traveler, and animal lover. Her cat, Myron, and her grandson, Philip, inspired her initial contributions to the ***Max and Myron*** series. Assisting her grandchildren to learn correct behavior as they grow continues to inspire her as she writes. Cats and kids can teach us so much. Wendy lives in northern California with her husband and new kitten. Maybe he will make an appearance soon!

Meet the Illustrator

Corie Barloggi is an educator, an author and an illustrator. She truly enjoys teaching elementary school while spending her spare time writing and illustrating children's books. Her favorite things in her life are her family, her two cats, her friends, baking and gardening. She feels that each child should be given the opportunity to have books in their life so they can learn to enjoy reading. She feels that by creating books children will enjoy and learn from is the beginning in helping them to become life-long readers.

www.ingramcontent.com/pod-product-compliance
Lightning Source LLC
Chambersburg PA
CBHW041801040426
42448CB00001B/3